Fueling Your New Home Sales Business

Making Strategic Contacts For More Sales & Referrals

Fueling Your New Home Sales Business

Making Strategic Contacts For More Sales & Referrals

Steve Hoffacker
CAPS, MCSP, MIRM

Fueling Your New Home Sales Business

Making Strategic Contacts For More Sales & Referrals

Cover photo by Steve Hoffacker.

ALL RIGHTS RESERVED.

© 2014 by Hoffacker Associates LLC
West Palm Beach, Florida, USA

ISBN: 978-0-692-32286-4

———

To make sales and build your new home sales business, you have two choices for finding and identifying people to meet and talk with about your new homes. You can wait for people to come to you that are produced from traditional and online marketing, or you can generate your own sales leads from people you know and those you will be meeting. The second alternative definitely is the more productive and sustainable for creating long-term success.

———

Other New Home Sales Books By Steve Hoffacker

To find additional books on new home sales written by Steve Hoffacker, visit http:stevehoffacker.com/newhomesalesbooks.html).

Titles are available in print (softbound) and as Kindle eBooks. They include:

"**Making The Grade:** *The A-B-C's Of Rating New Home Customers*"

"**Operation Discovery:** *Who, What, When, Where, & More In New Home Sales*"

"**Using Your Network:** *Making New Home Sales With People You Already Know*"

"**Making New Friends:** *Connecting With Strangers To Make More New Home Sales*"

"**Selling With Builders:** *How Realtors® Can Profit From Selling Builders' New Homes*"

"**Universal Design For Builders:** *Building & Selling Accessible, Safe & Comfortable New Homes*"

"**Creating A Great First Impression:** *Being An Effective New Home Sales Center Receptionist*"

Table Of Contents

Chapter	Page

Preface 11

1. **Stepping Out & Stepping Up** 19
   Continuing As You Are 19
   Taking Charge Of Your Success 20
   Recognizing How This Can Change 21
   Your Paradigm Shift 22

2. **Challenges Of Indirect Attraction** 25
   Why Most Marketing Is Passive 25
   Marketing Can Be Expensive 26
   Why Passive Marketing Prevails 28
   The Role Of The Internet 29
   Making The Transition 30

3. **Opportunities For Generating Traffic** 33
   Why It Matters 33
   Direct Contact Makes The Difference 34

A Financial Win 36
Start With Your Database 36
Your "Circle Of Contacts" 38

4. People You Already Know 39

A Great Place To Start 39
What Do You Say? 40
Getting Started 42
Making The Contact 43
Starting With The People Closest To You 45
Your Family — Immediate & Extended 46
Close & Well-Known Friends 47
Friends Of Friends & Other Contacts 48
Business Connections 50
People You See Regularly 55
People You Interact With Occasionally 56
Professional Services You Use 58
Sports & Recreation Acquaintances 59
Academic & Education Contacts 61
Summary Of People You Know 63
    Your family 64
    Close & well-known friends 65
    Friends of friends and other contacts 66
    Business connections 68
    People you see regularly 72
    People you interact with occasionally 73
    Professional services you use 75

Sports & recreation acquaintances 76
Academic & education contacts 78

5. People You Are Meeting 79

Changing Gears 79
Going For The Introduction 80
Getting Started 82
Making The Contact 84
Ineffective Or Inappropriate Contact 85
Actually Meeting Strangers 86
New/Occasional Places You Shop 88
Governmental Activities 91
Organizations & Groups 92
Schools & Education 93
Chance Encounters In Public 94
Medical Services 96
Real Estate & Related Services 96
Miscellaneous Sales Activities 97
Contractors 98
Recreational & Social Activities 99
Strategic Businesses & Professionals 100
Summary Of People You Can Meet 101
   New/occasional places you shop 102
   Governmental activities 103
   Organizations & groups 104
   Schools & education 105
   Public & chance encounters 105

Medical services 106
Real estate & related services 107
Miscellaneous sales activities 108
Contractors 108
Recreational & social activities 109
Transportation services/facilities 110
Food & dining 111
Professionals to meet 111

6. Now What? 113

Having A Plan 113
Putting Together A Plan 115
Keeping Your Priorities Straight 116
Now It's Up To You 118

Preface

As a new home sales representative, you need to have people to work with as you help them find the new home they are seeking and make money for you and your company.

Typically, you sit in a model home or staff a new home sales pavilion for your builder — or multiple builders, in the case of a central sales center.

One of the most exciting times of the day is when the front door opens and a new customer walks in.

Of course, the door can open with someone else besides a customer, such as a homeowner (with or without an issue to discuss with you), a supplier, an appraiser, or an employee from your company.

Nevertheless, you constantly are waiting for the door to open to give you a new opportunity to meet a potential purchaser and learn about how you can serve them.

Your inbox containing emails from people contacting you from your website is also something to get excited about.

Each time the phone rings, there is a possibility that it's someone wanting information on your new homes that you will later meet in person and have a more in-depth discussion about your homes.

Incoming phone calls can be for many different reasons from a variety of people, but the best ones are from people interested in talking with you about your new homes.

These are all traditional ways of producing traffic — someone walking into your office (regardless of how they learned about you and whether anyone else is with them), contacting you by email, or calling you.

As for people walking through your front door who are ready to learn about what you are offering, they could have been generated by a nearby directional or informational sign, they could have visited your website prior to their arrival, a friend of theirs could have told them about you, or they could be coming in with a Realtor®.

The same is true when people contact you by email or phone — they had to learn about you and how to contact before they could reach out to you.

This way of producing sales leads and traffic for your new home sales business is quite typical, but it also is very passive.

Preface

It works, but it is very difficult to project how many people might contact you or walk through your front door — from none to several a day.

The difficulty with a passive approach is that you have to wait for people to contact you — then you don't know how many there will be on any given day, how they will be spaced out (or bunched up) throughout the day, and what the relative quality of those leads will be in terms of interest level and ability to make a decision.

With conventional passive advertising or marketing, your message is sent out to the marketplace, and then it's up to people to see or hear your message, identify with it, determine that you have something they want to learn more about, and then contact you. Until that happens, you don't know who the person is that might have an interest in what you are offering. You just have to sit back and wait.

This is a very difficult and unpredictable way to sustain your business. You need to keep generating the same amount and quality of leads week after week and month after month to keep up your sales pace.

To expand your business using this approach, you would have to invest in more advertising opportunities — more ads, more sites or publications, bigger ads, and more frequent ones.

To be effective at having a sufficient number of people to talk with on a consistent basis to make sales, you need a dependable way of generating new leads that responds directly to your efforts.

Unlike placing more and more ads (after you determine where to actually advertise) and spending more and more money — which may indeed result in increased leads that you won't know about until they actually show up or contact you — you need an intentional, direct way of producing interested buyers.

This is where self-generation of leads comes in — also called various other names such as prospecting, proactive contact, cold-calling, canvassing, and farming. The objective is the same, regardless of what you call it.

You must commit to a program of involving people that you know and that you will meet into helping you build and sustain your new home sales business.

This book gives you ideas and strategies on where to begin a program of self-generation of sales leads — going way beyond the obvious, the easy, or even the comfortable.

It's not for everyone to try — just those who aren't satisfied with their current traffic numbers and are looking to go beyond what they are getting now.

Perhaps you have used such terms yourself, and you've undoubtedly heard other people talking about their "circle of influence" or "sphere of influence." We'll cover that and give you additional insight into how you can really grow the number available to you.

You won't be "using" your friendships as much as you'll be tapping into them.

Beyond that, there are so many other opportunities to engage people that you meet as you go about your normal routine. We'll discuss how they can help you, and you'll learn to look for people in places you likely hadn't thought of before.

I appreciate that you bought this book and that you are reading it — particularly because you have decided to be instrumental in producing the people to whom you will be selling new homes.

You will still make sales with people who walk into your sales center or contact you because they heard of what you are offering through conventional channels. However, as you read this book and put into practice the concepts I'll be giving you, you'll have a potential for creating new business that doesn't depend on traditional marketing.

You'll see that it is far more dependable and stronger for you that what you have been relying on until now.

As you use this book — and then put into practice what you learn here — you won't have to wait for people to contact you as would be the case otherwise. You'll be going out and finding the people who want to purchase a new home from you.

This is what is going to make you a stronger new home salesperson — regardless of whether others in your organization decide to use these strategies or not — that will sustain your business and even grow and expand it.

Now, let's get to work.

Fueling Your New Home Sales Business

Making Strategic Contacts For More Sales & Referrals

1

Stepping Out & Stepping Up

Continuing As You Are

You need people looking at and expressing an interest in your new homes in order to make sales and make money for you and your company.

However, if you do nothing more than what you are doing right now to generate traffic for your new home sales business, you only have two choices for making more sales and generating a larger income.

First, your company can run more ads, run larger ads, or run them in more places. That should generate more people contacting you and coming through your door.

You can join more social media sites, post more content, begin paying for premium accounts or ads, and invest more time this way.

Neither approach will necessarily improve the interest level or the ability of people to make decisions with you (quality), but it should improve the quantity.

The second way to make more sales is to increase your conversion ratio — closing a higher percentage of your sales presentations from your current traffic numbers than historically has been true.

Closing more sales without increasing the quality of your traffic will only allow you to improve slightly. At some point, you will have sold a new home to everyone that wanted what you offered and was capable of purchasing it.

You can only increase your closing percentage to a point — especially if the quality of your traffic remains fairly constant.

The rest of your traffic would remain a large group of people not interested in purchasing from you — at least not in the short-term.

Taking Charge Of Your Success

If you can only improve your sales production incrementally based on working with the traffic that your company's current marketing efforts are generating — and your ability to convert more of that traffic to closed transactions — the primary way open to you to make substantially more sales than what you are doing right now is by expanding both the number and quality of the people that visit you to look for a new home. That's what this book is all about.

There is a physical limit to the number of sales you can produce with your current traffic — even if you become much more efficient at closing. Therefore, you need to find a way — through your personal efforts — to bring more people into your sales center.

To do this, you're not going to be competing with your company as a lead generator. You're not going to running ads and doing other types of promotions and media marketing. You will be doing your own personal marketing — that only you can do —that complements and parallels what your company is doing.

You can be responsible for producing a very large share of your total traffic — even as much as all of it — and it will be a higher quality that what typical marketing produces. People will already know and like you, so the most difficult part of your sales presentation will not be an issue.

Recognizing How This Can Change

Since the most practical way of increasing sales (and your income) is by having more people to talk to who are in position to like what you are showing them and then able to make a favorable buying decision with you, you need a way to make this happen.

The advertising and marketing that your builder is doing — and presumably will continue to do — will generate a basic amount of traffic for you. Appreciate it, work with it, and make the sales that you can.

However, you need to take over and power your own lead generation system to insure that you have a sufficient quantity of people who are looking forward to meeting with you and who already understand something about what you are offering.

People like this are similar to a referral in the way they are predisposed to liking you and wanting to work with you because they, in essence, will have been referred by you.

What you are going to do — if you are up to the challenge — is to begin supplementing the traffic that normally arrives at your sales center or otherwise contacts you from traditional marketing and advertising from you or your builder.

Your Paradigm Shift

Starting as soon as you make the commitment to begin being your own traffic generator, you are going to look upon the traffic produced through passive traditional or conventional marketing — messages that require people to see or hear what you are saying, identify with them, and initiate the contact you with you — as something nice to have but nothing to rely or count on.

You are going to act as if the only people that you are going to have a chance to make sales with are those produced through your own efforts. This is how you are going to propel your new home sales business.

Thus, you are going to be very intentional about generating or producing the people that walk into your new home sales center. You quite likely will have talked to each of these people previously — as you met them if they were strangers or because you already knew them.

There is nothing passive about what you are going to be doing. It is direct marketing where you are taking your message to people, one-on-one and one-at-a-time.

You may not know everyone that you'll be talking to, and that's fine. We'll cover that as we go along. The important thing is that you are going to be having direct contact with them — often face-to-face.

This is the opposite of passive marketing where you never know who saw you message or has some interest in it until you actually hear from them. Even then you may have only partial contact information from them.

You are going to be talking with people you already know fairly well, people that you have met but don't know that much about them or haven't spoken to in a while, people that your friends and acquaintances introduce you to, people that you know by sight or name but have never been introduced to previously, and people who are total strangers to you when you meet them.

From this large, and ever-increasing group of people, you have the ability to create more interest and more sales than passive marketing is capable of doing — and at essentially no cost to you.

Other than a few minor expenses (such as an occasional cup of coffee, light meal, or transportation expenses), direct, intentional marketing is quite inexpensive.

We're going to look at where you can identify people that might be interested in owning what you have to offer — or referring interested people to you.

First, let's agree to rule out passive or indirect marketing as a serious possibility for intentionally or purposefully increasing your traffic numbers. That just is not its function.

2

Challenges Of Indirect Attraction

Why Most Marketing Is Passive

Most advertising and marketing — for new home sales as well as other businesses — is passive. The message is placed in a newspaper or other print publication, it is broadcast on TV or radio, it is displayed as a sign of some type, or it appears on the internet.

It is quite common, most people are familiar with it, and we see many instances of it throughout the day.

There are newspaper and magazine ads, online ads (including pop-up ads and pay-per-click), radio and TV commercials, billboards, directional and informational signs, vehicle wraps, bus benches, magnetic signs and placards on taxis and buses, direct mail postcards, catalogs (unsolicited and requested), flyers, contests, and giveaways — among many others.

With drive-by traffic (that technically isn't free because a flag or sign usually is used to attract someone's attention rather than just the fact that they see something they perceive as a model home), there usually isn't a direct expense associated with producing a sales lead or interested home shopper.

Social media (unless premium accounts or ads are used) are generally free to use.

However, with most forms of marketing, there typically is a charge for getting your advertising message out into the world or your local marketplace.

Marketing Can Be Expensive

Depending on the type of advertising message selected, when it is run, where it is used, and how often the ad is repeated, the expense can be quite substantial — especially considering the number of leads that respond to a particular message or campaign when the cost of that effort is broken down on a cost per lead basis.

The effectiveness of that campaign in terms of how many actual leads were produced, over what period of time, and the general quality of those leads all need to be factored in as well.

In essence, the question needs to be if the expense was justified for the results obtained.

To get a sense of how effective the advertising messages are doing in producing traffic, you need to determine how many people actually visited your sales center as a direct result of that particular campaign.

Then calculate the cost of producing each of those leads by dividing the total expense by the number of leads (including those with limited or very little interest as well as the ones who seemed to like what you offer).

When looking at just the number of sales that were produced (if any) or the quality leads that resulted from a particular marketing campaign, the relative expense often goes up dramatically. This needs to be considered when evaluating whether something like this should be done again.

Say for instance that a newspaper ad for one insertion costs $1,000 (this is just an example). If you get four people to respond to that message, that would be $250 per lead generated. If only two of those four liked what you offered or were capable of purchasing it, that would mean $500 per qualified lead. If one sale results — an exceptional return for just one ad and such a small response — that would be an advertising expenditure of $1,000 per sale.

If the ad cost was $2,000, $5,000, or $10,000, the ratios would change accordingly.

Why Passive Marketing Prevails

Even though there is an expense associated with traditional or conventional advertising and marketing (including agency costs, creative time, and actual placement of the messages), most builders continue to use it.

For one thing, it is easily understood as something that businesses generally do. In addition, consumers expect to see this type of advertising in some form.

It's also relatively simple to do. Create an ad and run it. While this may not be the easiest thing to do if you aren't artistic or don't have the help of an agency or marketing staff, it is still done by the preponderance of builders.

It can be managed in the office. An occasional trip to the newspaper office or advertising agency may be required, but quite often the planning details can be handled by them coming to your office or discussing it over the phone or online.

Even when other people need to get involved, they can be conferenced in by phone or live participation.

While there has been a shift away from print media in favor of being online, display ads are still being used and likely will continue.

The Role Of The Internet

While using the internet to promote your new homes and attract customers may seem different than placing an ad in the newspaper, it actually is quite similar — at least initially.

The internet is passive for you until someone connects with you — the same as is true for a newspaper ad or other form of indirect marketing where you don't know in advance specifically who is going to be receiving or responding to your message.

You likely have one or more websites — one that your builder maintains for the company, one that is specific to your new home community, or even one that you have just for yourself.

Still, this is passive because out of the millions of websites on the internet, someone has to search for what you are offering or otherwise land on your page. They may never get past that step of just looking — much the same as someone who looks at a newspaper ad and then moves on.

You can enhance your chances of someone finding your website through ads, pay-per-click, and optimization. If someone does visit your site and then emails you, you can begin a dialog with them although it may be just a series of emails back-and-forth.

Social media is similar in that you are posting content online with the idea that your followers and others might find something of interest and contact you. Keep in mind the hundreds of social media and blogging sites that exist and the millions of daily updates across those various sites.

Getting found is the biggest challenge. Creating and posting engaging content is also important. Then you want interested people to contact or follow you (with a way to connect with or contact them).

Making The Transition

All of us are familiar with indirect or passive marketing, advertising, and lead attraction. We have grown up with it, and we see it many times a day in some form for a variety of products. What we may not be as familiar with though is the opposite or converse approach — direct or intentional marketing.

Possibly you hadn't thought about or considered just how big of a process and involved it is to get someone to visit your website, contact you by phone or email, or walk through your front door when you are using traditional or conventional advertising or marketing.

Because of its passive and indirect nature, several steps are involved before you learn who has identified with your advertising message and feels that you have a new home that they might be interested in owning — or you actually meet and speak to someone who can purchase one of your new homes.

The other people who saw or heard your message remain unknown to you because they did not respond to your message. At some point, they may contact you, but until they do you won't know who was exposed to your message and ignored it.

Contrast that with talking to people intentionally and directly — and knowing who they are at the time.

Start by approaching and contacting people you already know because they are close friends, they are family, or you have some other type of relationship with them. They will talk with you simply because you know each other.

Even if it's been several months or even years since you last talked or saw each other — or you know them but not all that well — you still know each other enough for them to recognize your name or your face when you contact them or see them in-person.

After you let your friends and acquaintances know what you are doing and you provide them your current contact information, you can begin discussing the opportunities you offer and determine where there might be some level of interest.

The same is true with the people you are meeting for the first time — including people you might be familiar with by sight or reputation but have not actually had a conversation previously.

As you meet people and learn who they are, you introduce yourself and typically share a business card with them. Later, through a telephone conversation, email, letter, or meeting for coffee, you can explain more about what you do, how you can use their help, and determine their willingness to assist you.

Here, you are taking your message directly to people that you know, or that you meet in public, and that is the secret to propelling your new home sales business to success.

Use indirect marketing for what it can produce, but take charge of generating your own traffic by approaching people directly and intentionally.

3

Opportunities For Generating Traffic

Why It Matters

There is nothing inherently wrong with using indirect or passive marketing and advertising to produce traffic at your new home sales center except that there is a better, more consistent way of generating traffic.

As we have pointed out, passive lead generation relies on the people you want to reach with your message being receptive to seeing or hearing it, then doing so, then identifying with it as something that appeals to them, and then reaching out to you online, by phone, or through a personal visit to your sales center.

As a result, you get differing amounts of traffic — from none, just one or two, or even ten or more. You just never know from day-to-day how many people might show up or generally how interested they might be.

With intentional or direct lead generation, you are taking your message to specific people — whether that was your intent all along or it just came out in the conversation.

Either way, you will talking with people that you know (no matter how well) and that you can contact again.

Even if you are just meeting people for the first time, you still have a personal connection with them as opposed to their responding to an indirect advertising message.

The difference with an indirect message is that it isn't targeted to a specific person but rather a group of people that includes them. You don't know specifically who that person is until they contact you.

Direct Contact Makes The Difference

You might be thinking that when someone contacts you as a result of something they saw in the newspaper, on a billboard, or on your website, that you know who they are after they identify themselves to you or you learn who they are and begin your discovery process.

That is true, but the point is that you didn't know them *before* they contacted you — and if you did not capture their contact information — you still would not know who they are. Future conversations would be difficult.

People who contact you or visit your sales center that are prompted to do so through traditional marketing and advertising are assessing how well what you offer fits with what they are looking for in a new home and the reasons they are considering making a move.

When you contact specific people that you already know or that you meet, you learn about their needs and interest level before you even suggest that they visit your sales center. In this way, you are producing qualified traffic for yourself.

You can set a specific time for your friends or acquaintances to visit you so that you have more rhythm to the amount of traffic that might come in on any particular day. If no one else visits that day from ads or other marketing, you have the appointment or appointments that you set. If others come in as well, that just adds to your overall potential for that day.

This is how direct or intentional contact makes the difference. You take your message to a specific person, one-at-a-time rather than shotgunning or broadcasting it to a wide audience.

Then you have people to talk to in your sales office that already know you and already have expressed some interest in what you have to offer.

Also, they can refer you to their circle of contacts.

A Financial Win

Instead of trying to analyze which ads or advertising media work for you and where money should be allocated (including which marketing should be increased and by how much), direct contact marketing requires no significant analysis or outlay of capital.

Primarily you are talking about meeting someone for coffee, having a snack or dessert, and whatever transportation costs you might incur.

There is nothing to budget (or waiting until you have the funds) — just get started and do it.

Your company can continue doing the type of advertising and marketing that it typically does. You can then supplement or even replace traffic generated in that manner with what you are capable of doing yourself.

Start With Your Database

Everyone has a database, even if it's just numbers of frequently called people stored on their cellphone, a stack of collected business cards, or slips of paper with names and phone numbers written on them.

You likely have a computerized database that is synced with your smartphone.

For our purposes in this book — and the whole process of generating leads for yourself — it doesn't matter what type of a database you have or if it's formal or informal.

A formal one is that commonly referred to as a CRM or customer relationship manager. Examples of this are Outlook, ACT!, Maximizer, Gold Mine, Sales Simplicity, and Sales Force.

A less formal one is a Rolodex. While this contains the names and contact information of everyone whose business card you have, it can only be accessed alphabetically by the last name of the person unless you create some other type of filing system. Certainly it has no search capabilities the way a computerized database does.

An informal system includes a notebook with names and contact information written in it, a Christmas Card list, a stack of business cards rubber banded or clipped together (possibly even sorted into some type of commonality such as the event or function where they were collected, business type, or city), or a file box or three-ring binder with notecards or pages for each person.

Nevertheless, this database is going to be the base of your direct contact marketing efforts and will include everyone in it regardless of how you know them.

Your "Circle Of Contacts"

Some people like to refer to the group of people they know as their "Sphere of Influence" or "SOI." Personally, I think this is a very limiting term and does not allow for adding friends of friends or people you might meet over time. Seriously, how many people do we actually influence anyway?

"Circle of Friends" or "COF" is a similar tem that people use, but does this group include casual acquaintances or people from our past? Hard to say.

That's why I prefer the broader, more inclusive term "Circle of Contacts" ("COC") which includes everyone in your database and new ones that you will be adding.

In this book, we are going to be highlighting and focusing on your Circle of Contacts — as it is now and as it grows over time. This includes close friends, relatives, people from your past, customers, existing sales leads, casual acquaintances, former neighbors, people as you meet them, and people that anyone in your "Circle" introduces to you.

It doesn't matter how well or how long you know someone (or even if you know them right now in the case of people you will be meeting). This is where you are going to gain a supreme advantage over those who employ a simple "SOI" approach!

4

People You Already Know

A Great Place To Start

As you begin your self-generation program of identifying and producing interested people to look at your new homes, a great place to start is by contacting people you already know.

It doesn't matter how well you know someone or how long it's been since you've last contacted or spoke with them. It could be a distant cousin, someone you met at a business function a few years ago, someone you used to serve on a committee with, or a neighbor from several years ago.

The point is that you know their name and that they remember or know your name (maybe with a little prompting or reminding them of how you know each other).

Because of your acquaintance with people over the years — just a one-time meeting or someone you've known closely for a long time — the one thing that usually does not have to happen is selling yourself.

This typically is the first thing that needs to happen in making a sales presentation or building a relationship, but your friends and acquaintances know you and will listen to you without you needing to convince them of your intentions or why they should listen to you.

With this crucial initial step out of the way because your friends and acquaintances know you, you can move on to conveying your message.

What Do You Say?

You want to produce customers to look at your new homes and purchase from you so an easy place to begin is with people you already know because they know you also.

So, do you just call up or visit your friends and ask them if they want to buy a new home? No, it's not that direct, and you would go through your list way too fast this way.

The main thing you want to do is make sure they are aware that you are selling new homes — and what and where. This may be a new career direction for you since you last spoke to some of your friends or possibly worked with them in another business. Even if you have been selling new homes for a few years, they may not be aware of the builder you are working with now or the physical location where your office is located.

If they personally don't have a need for a new home, they likely will know someone that does or will agree to keep you in mind when they hear or learn of someone looking for a new home.

First, this is an educational mission — making sure that people you know realize what you are doing currently.

Then comes your story. You set up a time to meet over coffee or have them visit your sales center and discuss their needs in more detail — or the needs and interests of people that they know (you may know them also or they could be people that your friends will introduce to you).

Don't rush it! As you are notifying people of your current position, location, and contact information (you likely will send them a vCard or email your contact information), the conversation may naturally progress to their housing interest. If it doesn't, that's OK.

The initial reason for contacting your friends is for them to know where you are and what you are doing.

During subsequent conversations, you can share how you can use their help or learn about their particular needs and interests. Don't risk your friendship by making it seem that the only reason you are interested in them is if they can buy a new home from you.

As for specific questions, scenarios, and strategies for contacting your friends and acquaintances, consult my book "**Using Your Network:** *Making New Home Sales With People You Already Know*." There is no point in reprinting or discussing that information here since that resource exists — in print and as a Kindle eBook.

Getting Started

Because you are contacting your friends, relatives, people you see on a regular basis, and other people that you know, the actual words you use to have a conversation with them aren't as important as the act of contacting them.

That's why I recommend the "Using Your Network" book for ideas of what to say. Mainly, you just want to talk with the people you know,

First, determine if they are aware of what you're doing now. Second, make sure they can contact you as needed by providing your current email and cell phone number. Third, make sure you have their current and preferred email address and their cell phone number.

After you complete these steps and conduct any small talk about what each of you has been doing since your last conversation — along with the usual questions about health, family, and hobbies — you can see where the discussion leads. You want to leave the door open for another call, a meeting for coffee, golf or tennis, or a visit to your sales center — as appropriate.

As you go along, you will be setting appointments to meet with your friends and acquaintances — at their place of business or home, at a coffee shop, for recreation, or at your sales center — to discuss their interest in acquiring a new home, to discuss how you can use their help, and to learn who they can introduce you to that might like what you have available.

This is how you are going to begin creating traffic for your sales center.

Making The Contact

There are many ways to contact your friends and acquaintances. It can be as easy as talking to the neighbor when you both are outside or speaking to your relatives when they visit. There are many people you see every day or quite regularly that you know.

Looking for people to speak with that you already know will not be a challenge for you. If anything, reaching out to all of them is going to take some planning.

Because you are contacting people that you already know — some of them quite well — you can be fairly casual and informal. For instance, texting is never recommended for contacting someone you have never met, but it's fine to use with people that you know.

Emails are not recommended for the initial contact with someone when you are making an introduction. Nevertheless, emails — even ones sent from your smartphone without a fancy signature block — can serve your purposes quite well.

A general mailing just announcing your new position along with your business card might not get that much recognition or notice with people unfamiliar with you, but it can work for getting the word out to your friends — to be followed with a phone call or other type of contact.

As for reaching out by phone, you have the flexibility of calling people on their cell phone, at the office (or at the last business number you have for them), or at home (for those who still have landline home phone numbers). When you leave a voice message, you don't have to be as concerned about keeping it "all business" the way you would with someone you hadn't met yet.

Regardless of how you contact them — even if you drop by their home or office in person or see them during an impromptu meeting in public — you can cover a range of personal topics and subjects in addition to your main message. That's what friends and acquaintances do — they have conversations with each other about things that might be important to them.

At some point in the conversation, you can mention your current or new position (depending on how long you've been there and the length of time it's been since you last talked with a particular friend) and take it from there.

The notification of what you are doing now may be all that happens on your first contact, but eventually you are going to find out who might be interested in a new home (including friends of theirs that you may not know) and set up additional times to talk about what you are offering. From that, you will generate traffic for your new home sales center.

Starting With The People Closest To You

Without focusing on the actual content of what you want to say to your family and closest friends, the main thing you want to accomplish is making sure they know what you are doing and where.

You can approach them in a variety of ways, such as in-person the next time you see them if it's going to be relatively soon, a phone call, a personal visit to their home or office, or even a quick note, email, or text.

You want their help and support, but they won't be able to provide any assistance if they aren't even aware that you're selling new homes, the location, the builder, the name of the community, or the price point.

Your first contact is just informational — let them know what you are doing. They may have no idea that this is what you are doing so you need to tell them. If they know but hadn't thought about any help that you might need or want to build and expand your business, this opens the door for future conversations.

They may need a new home for themselves, they may know someone that has talked about looking for a new home, or they may not know of anyone looking for a new home.

That is immaterial at the point of initial contact. You just want your friends, relatives, acquaintances, and people you interact with on a regular basis to know what you are doing so you can talk about it later.

Your Family — Immediate & Extended

As for the people you want to be sure you contact and notify that are the closest to you, start with your **immediate family** (regardless of where they currently live) — brothers, sisters, parents, and stepsiblings. If your children or stepchildren are old enough to be employed or on their own, add them.

Include your **close relatives** (aunts, uncles, grandparents, cousins, "unofficial" aunts and uncles — people not related to you that you still address as aunt or uncle or consider them in that role, children of such aunts and uncles that you refer to "unofficially" as cousins, and neighbors or family friends whom you have adopted as "grandparents").

Distant relatives are cousins, aunts, and uncles you don't see that often, or those one or two generations removed (such as a great-aunt or second-cousin).

You also want to include family members who are related to you through **marriage**, including in-laws, stepparents' family, and your spouses' cousins, uncles, aunts, and grandparents (including the unofficial ones who are regarded as family and addressed that way).

If you have children who are married, include their spouse's families also.

Close & Well-Known Friends

After contacting your close family — or while you're doing that — you also want to make sure that the people you know quite well and those you've known the longest are aware of what you're doing so they can provide assistance when you request it.

Start by talking with the **residential neighbors** around

you on your street or building and the **business neighbors** that are near your sales center or corporate office.

Speaking of neighbors, be sure to include those from **former neighborhoods** that still live where they did or those you know how to contact.

Friends are a big part of your network, so start with your **close friends** — the ones that you text, go out with socially, see at church, or talk with several times a week. They may already know what you're doing, but maybe it hasn't come up or been discussed specifically.

Add in other friends that aren't as close to you but still well known to you. They may live in your town or city, or they could be in other parts of the country or world.

Friends Of Friends & Other Contacts

Don't forget people who aren't as well known to you such as **acquaintances** (people you have met or spoken with once or twice that you met on your own or through another friend or family member).

Friends (and relatives) of friends or **"downline" friends** are those people that you may not know yet, but your friends and acquaintances will introduce you to the people they are close to and their relatives so that it's the same as if you already knew them. This can be a very large circle of contacts for you.

Don't overlook the **lists**.

The people on these lists may be included in the friends and relatives category already, but this is a way of double-checking to make sure you haven't overlooked anyone who should know what you are doing. This includes your **holiday card list** (if you still mail cards, or perhaps your email list), **graduation invitation list** (for high school and college when this applies), a **wedding or engagement announcement list** (when applicable), and an invitation list for a **housewarming**, **birthday celebration**, **anniversary**, or **major party**.

Look at where you've been over the years: military, college, and organizations.

Look at close relationships you had in the **military** (basic training as well as work assignments after that), **churches** or **places of worship** you attend now or used to attend, **committees** you serve on or chair (or did previously), **organizations** you belong to now or did and those you have supported, **charities** and **non-profit groups** you helped (as a volunteer, committee or board member, or contributor), and **activities** that your kids participate in now or did at one time (school, scouting, sports, or hobbies) where you know or did know the adults who were active.

Some of these people you are going to know better than others, but you had shared experiences with them. Make sure they know what you are doing now so you can enlist their help later.

Finally, there are your **online friends** that you have met through **social media sites**, **blogs** that you write or follow, **forums** you participate in, or people who follow or interact with you (daily if not more often) and where you have developed a friendship.

Business Connections

Friends and family are a great place to begin reaching out to establish your personal network, and you should add your strong business connections also — to make sure they know what you are doing (for those you are not already interacting with in your sales center or neighborhood) and to request their help in generating referrals and interest among the people they know.

There could be some overlap because some of your business colleagues might be close friends or ones you socialize with or work with on various committee on which you serve, or organizations where you have a membership.

The important thing is not where you know someone or what category you might sort them in — you just want to include and contact as many people as possible that you already know.

Start with people that you know fairly well from comings and goings in and around your sales center (current or former one with the same or different company), office building where your corporate office is, or places where you have made presentations or held business functions.

This includes **sales and office assistants, receptionists, virtual assistants, office staff,** and **consultants** that are currently working or have previously worked (**former staff**) in your sales center or at the main office. They obviously know what you are doing so you want to lay the groundwork for referrals and meeting friends and contacts that they have.

Depending on the size or layout of your new home community, you might also have **security personnel, amenity staff, landscaping crews,** and **maintenance personnel** that you should include. Add to that people who have worked in those positions previously (**past employees**) and **previous applicants** who were not hired for sales, office, and maintenance positions.

If your company contracts for these **business services** from a private company rather than provide them in-house, reach out to those you know in those offices.

Look at your **present customers** and **homeowners** (or

renters in your community) for people they might know that they are willing to tell you about or allow you to contact. The same is true of people you've worked with in the past at **previous communities** or who have purchased elsewhere ("**lost sales**").

Don't forget to include the **real estate sales professionals** (including **Realtors**®) that you know (in your local market and nearby), **real estate brokers**, **office managers** and **assistants** at brokerage offices, **stagers**, **appraisers**, **home inspectors**, **surveyors**, **mortgage brokers, lenders**, and **title companies**.

Make a special point of connecting with the **listing agents** of homes for sale in your new home community and surrounding streets — especially those you already know. For those unfamiliar to you, it won't be hard to meet them since you have a common neighborhood and homes to discuss.

Homeowners using **remodeling contractors** who are familiar to you gives you a reason to approach both the remodeler and the homeowner.

Those homeowners (or renters) who are moving into or out of your community — who don't do the moving themselves — may use the services of a **moving company** that you know. You can talk with them right in your community — or go to their office once you see who they are.

Search your **database**, **CRM**, **Rolodex**, stack of **business cards**, **slips of paper**, **membership directories**, and anyplace else you may have the names and contact information of people recorded that you should tell about what you are doing. Many of those name may already have been included in other categories, but make sure no one is overlooked.

Think of **restaurants**, **hotels**, **resorts**, or **conference centers** (local or not) where you and your company have business meetings, get-togethers, and training events.

Be sure to include all of the people who help you and your company build and deliver your new homes to your customers. Start with your **market research firms**, **land planners**, **engineers**, **marketing agencies**, **PR firms**, **consultants**, **architects**, **design professionals**, **interior designer**, **decorators**, and **landscape architects**. Then include the **trade contractors** (the people you see on the jobsite plus those you know or speak with in their office).

Regardless of the type of home you build, or the price point, there are certain tradespeople that are going to be involved in the construction of your homes. Then there may be others as well, depending on the specific features, fixtures, and finishes you include or have installed.

This is not meant to be an exhaustive list of people who may be involved in the construction of your homes, but look to the **trade partners** where you know and recognize people, such as **carpenters** (rough, finish, and trim), **framers, cement finishers, flatwork contractors**, masons, roofers, HVAC, electricians, plumbers, drywallers, painters, tile setters, cabinet installers, countertop installers, flooring contractors, **lighting contractors, low voltage electrical contractors**, elevator or **special equipment installers**, and **other specialty contractors**.

Look to other that you see on your jobsites also, such as **building inspectors, building materials delivery, concrete delivery, equipment operators, laborers, trash removal, landscapers, utility installers**, and **cleaning services** (people who prepare your new homes prior to delivery).

In short, don't overlook speaking with anyone you see on the jobsite about their own needs or those of people that they know who might be interested in looking at or owning one of your new homes.

This is a very special group of people to reach out to and engage because they are intimately familiar with what you offer.

One other type of business contacts and connections is through the organizations and associations you belong to and attend, such as **groups for sales professionals, mastermind groups, networking groups, chambers of commerce, civic organizations, home builders** association, **sales and marketing council**, and similar groups where are least one precept of the group is devoted to helping you identify and obtain new sales leads.

People You See Regularly

Aside from several people already mentioned that you see on a regular basis (neighbors, customers, staff, associates, contractors, homeowners, Realtors®, family, close friends, and others), there are many other people you encounter daily, weekly, or frequently.

In no certain order of importance or frequency of people that you might see often, you likely have a good relationship with **delivery** people, such as **parcel delivery**, **regular mail**, **bottled water service**, **coffee service**, express delivery, and **messenger/courier services**.

Depending on your morning schedule, you may have a daily or regular stop at a **coffee**, **donut**, **fast food**, **bagel shop**, **convenience store**, or **a newsstand**.

If you attend religious services, then once a week or so, you'll see your **clergy** and people in your **congregation**.

If you have children or serve as an adult volunteer or leader, there are weekly **scout troop** meetings and monthly award and camping programs. If you serve as a

coach, **mentor**, **tutor**, or **volunteer** for youth sports, youth clubs, or academics, you have regular interaction with the children's parents.

At home or at your sales center (or both), you'll see service personnel on a weekly or monthly basis for **pool service, pest control, housekeeper/office cleaning, landscapers/lawn service/plant service**. Some utilities are monitored electronically, but you might see **meter readers** once a month.

Finally, there are many personal services that you or members of your family might use as often as daily. They include the **gym/spa, personal trainer, pet sitting/grooming, hair stylist, nail technician, barber shop, dry cleaners, tailors/alterations**, and **child care/after care**. You may also have **sitters** come to your home for your children or your pets.

People You Interact With Occasionally

In addition to those people you know quite well and those you see on a regular basis (even if you don't know them that well beyond the business relationship you have with them), there are many others that you see occasionally.

While infrequent, you will see some people more often than others. There are many different types of businesses that fall into this category.

Depending on how often your computer, TV, internet connection, phone line, appliances, air conditioner or furnace, and water and electric lines (at home on in your sales center) need service or attention, you will see your **computer repair/IT technician, satellite or cable TV company, internet service technician, copier service, HVAC technician, appliance repair, plumber,** or **electrician** on a semi-regular or occasional basis. You might also have a **handyman** that helps out with repairs at home or at your sales center.

For your car, you likely take it for occasional **service, oil changes**, and **tire maintenance**. You may even use a **detailing** or **car wash and wax** service.

Remember people that you know and encounter as you shop in the marketplace for various items or services for your home, businesses, car, or hobbies (**merchants and stores**). These are people that you know by name and that you've had conversations with in the past when you have been in their establishment or perhaps seen them in public someplace.

More specifically, the merchant and store category includes **clothing, shoes, jewelry and accessories, office supplies, automobile dealers** (the actual showroom or the parts or service departments), **auto accessories, boat or water craft dealers, sporting goods, florists/gift baskets, printers/signs, home improvement centers, bookstores, grocery stores, convenience stores, liquor** stores/wine shops, appliances and TVs, pharmacies, technology, furniture/home furnishings, and similar types of establishments.

Don't forget **restaurants** (dine-in or takeout), **pizza shops** (takeout or delivery), **sandwich shops, food trucks, fast food places,** and **street vendors** or **kiosks** that you frequent on a fairly regular basis where you and the employees, managers, and staff know each other well enough to have more than just a casual conversation when you visit.

If you own an RV and keep it at a **storage facility**, or use a **marina** for your boat, those are places you likely see some of the same faces each time you visit (employees or fellow owners). You might also use a storage facility for bulky, seasonal, or little-used household items.

Professional Services You Use

All of us interact with **professionals** and their **office staff** from time-to-time — some more frequently than others.

You might be looking for a new provider for some of these services, but begin with the professionals you have been using. They have benefitted from your patronage and should be willing to help you. If they have a personal need for a new home (and one such as you offer), that's great. Otherwise, they may be able to suggest people for you to meet.

This category includes medical professionals such as **doctors**, **nurses**, **optometrists**, **dentists**, **dental technicians**, **therapists**, **physician assistants**, **pharmacists**, and **pharmacy technicians**. If you have a pet, include **veterinarians**.

Either personally, or through your business, you likely will use the services of an **accountant**, **attorney**, **paralegal**, **notary**, **bank/credit union**, **insurance agent**, and **financial planner**.

Sports & Recreation Acquaintances

As you and your family engage in sports, recreation, hobbies, and related activities, there are many ways and opportunities to interact with people that you know. Some you will know very well because you see them everytime you participate in that activity, and others you will know less well — having met them just once or just seeing them occasionally.

In this category, we'll refer to everyone as "acquaintances" even though some are much more familiar and closer contacts than that.

Depending on the activity, and who is doing it (you, you and your spouse or partner, your kids, or the whole family), you might see the same people or group of people you know as often as every time. For others it could be just once or twice a season.

Let's start with **sports or activities** that you personally participate in or play. Pick the applicable ones for yourself from the following list: **tennis, racquetball, golf, softball, rugby, soccer, hockey, running, jogging, paddleboarding, surfing** (wave and wind), **canoeing, kayaking, boating, fishing, skiing** (snow and water), **skating** (ice and roller), **motocross, auto rallies/racing, basketball, touch/flag football, biking** (hard surface and mountain), **camping, skeet/target shooting, hunting, bowling,** and **walking.** There could be other activities as well, but you get the idea. There must be many familiar people that you will see as you participate in these activities.

Also, think of the people you know — no matter how well you know them or how regularly you see them — that share your hobbies and attend **dog shows, horse shows and events, car meets and exhibitions, flower shows, RC planes/cars clubs, model clubs, railroading clubs, photography clubs, gardening clubs,** and similar types of events or meetings.

Over time, as new members join these groups, clubs, or activities, you will meet additional people.

Look at people you may know because of the activities of other members of your family. If you have children, they may participate in **youth/school baseball**, **softball**, **football**, **basketball**, **hockey**, **BMX**, **lacrosse**, **rugby**, or other activities where you will know their coaches, teachers, assistants, league officials, and the parents of some of the other children.

Your spouse or partner may engage in some sports or recreational activities separately from you, and you may know people that way as well.

Don't forget your **circle of fans** of your local or nearby professional sports teams that you support, **old/former teammates** from high school, college, or professional (depending on how long ago this was), and fellow **booster club members** for teams you support.

Academic & Education Contacts

Over the years you have spent numerous hours in the classroom at **schools** and **seminars** you have attended, and you have met many people along the way at schools your **children** attend.

Look at people that you have met in a formal academic setting at one or more schools you attended (coursework or degree program) as well as **continuing education courses**, **seminars**, **professional education sessions**, **certification programs**, **workshops**, and other learning opportunities — **instructors**, **faculty**, **facilitators**,

assistants, administrators, office staff, fellow students/ classmates, and others.

Depending on how long ago it was that you attended school, the faculty and staff you knew while you were there might still be employed there or connected with the school.

You might be part of a **sorority or fraternity** where you are still active or have contacts. You might have been inducted in one or more **honor societies** that still have functions or a membership directory.

If your school has several alumni and graduates living in your area, there should be one or more **alumni groups** that have been formed to host various functions throughout the year.

As you have attended **sales seminars, sales rallies, professional designation/certification programs**, or **continuing education courses** outside your company, you likely have met the instructors and fellow professionals that can help you build your business.

If you have children in school now, you will know their **teachers**, **coaches**, some of the **staff** and **administration**, and some of the **other parents**. You will know people through **PTA** (or a similarly named parent group) meetings, functions, and fund-raisers. You might even serve on or chair a committee.

If your kids no longer attend that school (or any school), but the teachers or others you knew at that time are still there, you still have the ability to contact them.

Summary Of People You Know

In the preceding pages, I gave you categories of many people that you likely know in some capacity (from very well to casual acquaintances) that you should reach out to and engage — making sure they know what you are doing, where you are doing it, and that at some point you are going to want their help in promoting your community and sending people to you or introducing you to their contacts.

Then, it's just a matter of deciding which type of contact is appropriate for each person you want to engage — email, text, informal note, mailing, personal letter, phone call, or personal visit (to their home, office, function, meeting, or a place you know they will be). You might even have chance meetings with many of your friends as you see them in a store, at the gas station, church, sporting event, or other public place.

Here, in outline form are the many categories and types of individuals that you will want to engage as you let your family, friends, and acquaintances know what you are doing, build interest in your new homes, and generate leads for you to talk to about your offerings — either them personally or people they will share with you.

This is not meant to be an exhaustive list, but it is extensive.

Next to each line item, you might mark whether this is someone you have already talked with, it's someone that you intend to engage, or it's not high on your list right now. Nevertheless, this is your list, and this represents just people that you know.

In the next chapter, we'll look at meeting people who are strangers to you at this moment.

- **Your family**
  - **Immediate family**
    - Brothers
    - Sisters
    - Stepsiblings
    - Parents
    - Stepparents
    - Children
    - Stepchildren
  - **Close relatives**
    - Aunts
    - Uncles
    - Grandparents
    - Cousins
    - "Unofficial" aunts
    - "Unofficial" uncles

- o "Unofficial" cousins
- o "Adopted" grandparents
- **Distant relatives**
  - o First cousins
  - o Second-cousins
  - o Third generation cousins
  - o Aunts
  - o Uncles
  - o Great-aunts
  - o Great uncles
- **Family members through marriage**
  - o In-laws
  - o Stepparent's family
  - o Spouse's cousins
  - o Spouse's uncles and aunts
  - o Spouse's grandparents
  - o Spouse's "unofficial" relatives
  - o Spouse's families of married children

- <u>**Close & well-known friends**</u>
  - **Residential neighbors**
    - o People on your street or in your building
    - o Others you know in your community
  - **Business neighbors**
    - o Near your sales center
    - o Tenants in same building as your main office

- Near your corporate or main office
- **Former neighbors**
  - People that lived next to or across from you
  - Others you knew on your street or building
- **Close friends**
  - Those you see/talk with several times a week
  - Others you know very well (local or not)

- **Friends of friends and other contacts**
  - **Acquaintances**
    - People you have met on your own
    - People met through a friend or relative
  - **Friends of friends**
    - Friends of your relatives
    - Acquaintances of people you know
    - Relatives of theirs you don't know
  - **Lists** (for people not included elsewhere)
    - Holiday card list
    - Graduation invitation list
    - Wedding or engagement announcement list
    - Birthday celebration or anniversary invitations
    - Housewarming or major party invitation list
  - **Military service**
    - Basic training
    - Deployments and work assignments

- **College**
    - Roommates
    - Dormitory friends
    - Sorority/fraternity members and contacts
    - Clubs, honor societies, and organizations
- **Churches/places of worship**
    - Current attendance
    - Former attendance
    - Committees or small groups
- **Committees**
    - Current or previously served on
    - Chaired
- **Organizations**
    - Current and past memberships
    - Committees
- **Charities**
    - Boards and committees
    - Other volunteer work
- **Other non-profit groups**
- **Youth activities** (where you knew the adults)
    - School
    - Scouting
    - Sports
    - Hobbies

- **Online friends**
  - Social media connections
  - Blogs you write or follow
  - Forum sites
  - People who follow or interact with you
- **Business connections**
  - **Your company**
    - Sales assistants
    - Office staff
    - Receptionists
    - Virtual assistants
    - Consultants
    - Former staff
    - Previous applicants
  - **Your new home community**
    - Security personnel
    - Amenity staff (golf, club, tennis, food/beverage)
    - Landscaping crews
    - Maintenance personnel
    - Firms who provide these services contractually
  - **Purchaser referrals**
    - Present customers
    - Homeowners/renters in your community
    - Homeowners in previous communities
    - "Lost sales"

- **Real estate sales and related professionals**
    - Realtors® (in your local market and elsewhere)
    - Listed properties in your new home community
    - Listed properties nearby
    - Real estate brokers
    - Brokerage office managers
    - Real estate sales assistants
    - Stagers
    - Appraisers
    - Home inspectors
    - Surveyors
    - Mortgage brokers
    - Lenders
    - Title companies
    - Moving companies
- **Remodeling contractors** (for current owners)
- **Your database**
    - CRM
    - Rolodex
    - Stack of business cards
    - Slips of paper
    - Directories
- **Local meeting locations for your company**
    - Restaurants
    - Hotels
    - Resorts

- Conference centers
- **Creative consultants**
  - Market research firms
  - Consultants
  - Engineers
  - Marketing agencies
  - PR firms
  - Architects
  - Land planners
  - Design professionals
  - Interior designers
  - Decorators
  - Landscape architects
- **Trade contractors** (people you see on site plus those you know or speak with in their offices)
  - Carpenters (rough, finish, and trim)
  - Framers
  - Cement finishers and flatwork contractors
  - Masons
  - Roofers
  - HVAC
  - Electricians
  - Plumbers
  - Drywallers
  - Painters
  - Tile setters
  - Cabinet installers

- Countertop installers
  - Flooring contractors
  - Lighting contractors
  - Low voltage electrical contractors
  - Elevator or special equipment installers
  - Other specialty contractors
- **Other construction contacts**
  - Building inspectors
  - Building materials delivery
  - Concrete delivery
  - Equipment operators
  - Laborers
  - Trash removal
  - Landscapers
  - Cleaning services
  - Utility installers
- **Networking organizations and associations**
  - Groups for sales professionals
  - Mastermind groups
  - Networking groups
  - Chambers of commerce
  - Civic organizations
  - Home builders association
  - Sales and marketing council
  - Similar groups devoted to helping you identify and obtain new sales leads

- **People you see regularly**
  - **Delivery people**
    - Parcel delivery
    - Regular mail
    - Bottled water service
    - Coffee service
    - Express delivery
    - Messenger/courier services
  - **Morning stops**
    - Coffee
    - Donuts
    - Fast food
    - Bagel shop
    - Convenience store
    - Newsstand
  - **Religious services**
    - Clergy
    - Congregation
    - Adult Bible study, small groups, or discussions
    - Volunteer
  - **Youth group volunteer, leader, or coach** (parent and adult interaction)
    - Scout troop meetings
    - Monthly award programs
    - Camping outings
    - "Sunday School" teacher

- Hobby or activity club instructor
- Youth sports coach
- Academic mentor or tutor

- **Cleaning and maintenance personnel** (at home or your sales center/models)
  - Pool service
  - Pest control
  - Housekeeper/office cleaning
  - Landscapers/lawn service/plant service
  - Meter readers

- **Personal services**
  - Gym/spa
  - Personal trainer
  - Pet sitting/grooming/boarding
  - Hair stylist
  - Nail technician
  - Barber shop
  - Dry cleaners
  - Tailors/alterations
  - Child care/after care/sitters

- <u>**People you interact with occasionally**</u>
  - **Repair and service**
    - Computer repair/IT technician
    - Satellite or cable TV company
    - Internet service technician
    - Copier service
    - HVAC technician

- Appliance repair
- Plumber
- Electrician
- Handyman
- Auto service/repairs (including tires)
- Oil changes
- Car wash/wax/detailing

- **Merchants and stores**
  - Clothing
  - Shoes
  - Jewelry and accessories
  - Office supplies
  - Automobile dealers (showroom, parts, service)
  - Automotive accessories
  - Boat or water craft dealer
  - Sporting goods
  - Florists/gift baskets
  - Printers/signs
  - Home improvement centers
  - Appliances and TVs
  - Bookstores
  - Technology
  - Furniture/home furnishings
  - Grocery stores
  - Convenience stores
  - Liquor stores/wine shops
  - Pharmacies
  - Other stores and merchants

- **Dining**
    - Restaurants (dine-in or takeout)
    - Pizza shops (takeout or delivery)
    - Sandwich shops
    - Fast food places
    - Food trucks
    - Street vendors/kiosks
- **Storage facility**
    - RV storage or lot
    - Marina
    - Warehouse (seasonal, personal, household items)
- **Professional services you use**
    - Doctors
    - Nurses
    - Optometrists
    - Dentists
    - Dental technicians
    - Therapists
    - Physician assistants
    - Pharmacists
    - Pharmacy technicians
    - Veterinarians.
    - Accountant
    - Attorney
    - Paralegal
    - Notary
    - Your banker or credit union

- o Insurance agents
- o Financial planner
- **Sports & recreation acquaintances**
  - **Sports and activities you personally do**
    - o Tennis
    - o Racquetball
    - o Golf
    - o Softball
    - o Rugby
    - o Soccer
    - o Hockey
    - o Running
    - o Jogging
    - o Paddleboarding
    - o Surfing (wave, wind)
    - o Canoeing
    - o Kayaking
    - o Boating
    - o Fishing
    - o Skiing (snow, water)
    - o Skating (ice, roller)
    - o Motocross
    - o Auto rallies/racing
    - o Basketball
    - o Touch/flag football
    - o Biking (hard surface, mountain)
    - o Camping

- Skeet/target shooting
- Hunting
- Bowling
- Walking
- Other activities

- **Hobbies & other activities**
  - Dog shows
  - Horse shows and events
  - Car meets and exhibitions
  - Flower shows
  - RC planes/cars clubs
  - Model clubs
  - Railroading clubs
  - Photography clubs
  - Gardening clubs
  - Similar types of events or meetings

- **Activities of other family members**
  - Youth/school baseball
  - Youth/school softball
  - Youth/school football
  - Youth/school basketball
  - Youth/school hockey
  - Youth BMX
  - Youth/school lacrosse
  - Youth/school rugby
  - Youth/school hobbies and clubs
  - Your spouse's/partner's sports and activities

- **Fan connections**
    - Your circle of fans for your local team or teams
    - Old/former teammates
    - Fellow booster club members
- **Academic & education contacts**
    - **Schools, seminars and continuing education**
        - Instructors
        - Faculty
        - Administrators
        - Facilitators
        - Assistants
        - Office staff
        - Fellow students/classmates
        - Others
    - **Membership groups**
        - Sorority or fraternity
        - Honor societies
        - Alumni groups
    - **Your children's schools**
        - Teachers
        - Staff
        - Administration
        - Coaches
        - Assistants
        - Other parents
        - PTA (or other parent group)

5

People You Are Meeting

Changing Gears

Now that you have a good grasp for contacting and engaging people that you already know — to make sure they are aware of what you are doing and to have a conversation with them about how they or someone that they know might own one of your new homes — it's time to expand your focus to people unfamiliar to you.

This group of people that you don't know might be total strangers that you encounter for the first time as you go about your daily living, they could be people that you know by sight but have never spoken to, or they could be people that are associated with businesses that you intend to engage.

Nevertheless, you have two fantastic ways to build your business and fuel the creation of new sales leads and onsite traffic. You can contact and work with people that you already know — such as those we have been examining in the previous chapter — or you can meet new people.

Some new home salespeople even prefer to start their proactive, intentional contact of new sales leads by contacting strangers because they find that easier than reaching out to people that they know.

They don't want to create the impression among their friends and relatives that they are needy. While there is absolutely nothing wrong in asking for help — because we are internally wired to be able to offer assistance to each other — some salespeople just prefer to start their lead generation program by working with strangers.

There is no right or wrong way to begin reaching out to people except for not doing it at all or attempting to make things happen too quickly.

Going For The Introduction

When you approach your relatives, friends, and acquaintances about helping you to build your business, you don't need to sell yourself to them or introduce yourself first. This is typically an initial step in selling, but they know who you and will believe what you are telling them — when they agree to visit your sales center (because you have invited them to see what you offer) or they offer to introduce you to people in their circles that you don't know.

When you are meeting total strangers or people you have never formally met before, you must begin with the introduction. Sometimes that's as far as the conversation will go.

The first rule of successful selling is to sell yourself first. For anything except a routine purchase, the customer must like and trust you before they will be willing to consider doing business with you.

This all begins with an introduction. It doesn't need to be anything fancy or rehearsed. Tell them who you are and what you do. Make it sound like any other introduction between two people meeting for the first time and not like you are going to ask them to purchase a home from you in the next sentence.

After your new acquaintance knows your name, you then have the ability to contact them and pursue a longer discussion — one that lead to a more in-depth discussion of what you offer and what they might be looking for in a new home, if indeed they are interested in acquiring a new home.

For those people you meet who are not interested in getting a new home (for a variety of reasons, such as the price, location, style of a new home, or being happy with what they have now), they may have friends and acquaintances they will mention or introduce to you.

As for specific questions, scenarios, and strategies for approaching strangers or carrying on a conversation with people you are meeting for the first time, refer to my book "**Making New Friends:** *Connecting With Strangers To Make More New Home Sales.*" There is no point in reprinting or discussing that information here since that resource exists.

Getting Started

Because you are working with a very large potential of people you don't know presently, there are many ways to begin. Start by just going about your normal daily activities. Be open to the possibility of seeing and engaging new people at various places you go, or activities you undertake away from the office each day, without being obsessed by it. Let it happen.

You'll encounter people you don't know or don't normally see at your morning coffee stop, lunch break, gas station or convenience store on the way home, grocery store or takeout restaurant to get items for dinner, and any place you may stop to pick up something you need for yourself or someone at home. Of course there are many more possibilities.

On your day off, you can make it a point of running errands or shopping at stores or locations you might not normally visit. Eat lunch or grab a coffee at a new location to see whom you might meet.

Make a list of offices and businesses that you want to visit that are within your general market area — attorneys, accountants, real estate offices, retail locations, street vendors, kiosks, newsstands, and other types of businesses. Then make a plan to begin visiting them and meeting at least one person at each location. Remember the introduction comes first, then the message.

Search online for items that you are thinking of purchasing, and then call the local stores that have that item. While you are interested in eventually purchasing the item you are interested in, you are more concerned initially with meeting new people — first on the phone and then in-person when you visit that establishment.

Engage people who call you trying to make a sale, set an appointment, or solicit a donation. They won't be expecting you to turn the tables on them, but go for it. You have nothing to lose. You likely will get pushback or a "no," but what if there is some interest?

Just be in the world — at sporting events, standing in line, getting gas for your car, or most any other activity where there are other people present — and be open to the possibility of meeting someone new.

Making The Contact

To make the initial contact with someone you are seeing or speaking to for the first time, this takes more planning and awareness than when you are talking with people that you already know. Since you don't know who these people are until you actually see, meet. and engage them, there are no advance phone calls, notes, letters, emails, or texts that you can send to let people know what you are doing and to pave the way for future conversations and referrals.

As you are just going about your daily activities, you are going to be around hundreds of other people in the course of a year that you are capable of speaking with and engaging.

This is not just a matter of standing on the corner and passing out flyers of business cards to everyone walking by. In fact, there has to be a personal connection first.

Don't set time limits or quotas on your activity. Don't go into a public area with the idea that you will meet so many people or collect so many business cards. Don't set an amount of people that you want to meet in 15, 30, or 60 minutes. Just be open to engaging someone around you — one at a time.

Remember that you are going for for the introduction first and then enough contact information (at least a name and phone number) for you to speak to them again — as well as permission from them to do so.

Ineffective Or Inappropriate Contact

Be careful of the methods employed to contact and engage people you do not know. What works for friends and acquaintances may be totally ineffective or inappropriate to use with strangers and those you want to approach.

Passing out business cards in public or at an event, without knowing who took one (and how to get back in touch with them to pursue a conversation), does you little good unless that person has an immediate need for your homes and calls or emails you from just having your card.

While texting can work for your close circle of contacts, it is never recommended for contacting someone you have never met.

Similarly, emails are not recommended for the initial contact with someone when you are making an introduction.

A general mailing just announcing your new position along with your business card can work for getting the word out to your friends but might not get that much recognition or notice with people unfamiliar with you.

As for reaching out by phone, avoid using someone's cell phone for the initial contact unless it is advertised on their website, it's mentioned on their voice mail message, or someone in their office gave it to you. Still, this contact might be a little informal for the initial introduction.

If you decide to leave a voice message — since they won't know who you are — identify yourself and your company as someone who would like to meet them (because you are neighbors or have a general affinity for the area) and that you will call back. Do not leave a number, and do not leave additional messages if you call again and get the voice mail.

Just ask yourself if the reverse was happening — if someone that you didn't know and weren't sure if you wanted to know was trying to meet you to ask for your help — what would you consider to be an appropriate first contact?

Actually Meeting Strangers

Not everyone that you meet for the first time will be a total stranger to you in the sense that you don't know who they are by face, name, or reputation. It does mean that you have never been introduced to them and that you have never spoken — except possibly a cordial "hello" or smile you have exchanged with them when you see them occasionally.

In addition to people that you recognize and know who they are **by sight** because you sometimes see them in public (but have never formally met or had a conversation) — or because you have seen them on TV, in print articles, or on social media — you may also **know their name** from seeing it or hearing it. You might also belong to the **same group or organization** without ever having actually met previously.

Perhaps, you don't know them by name or even sight, but you know the **name of a business** that you want to contact, and you will eventually meet this person or persons.

You may also decide to focus on a **particular location** like your community, an office building, a shopping plaza, businesses at an intersection, or a specific block or neighborhood.

Lastly, there are people who are **total strangers** that you will meet for the first time at various places — some places that intentionally you go to or visit because you recognize that there is a good possibility that there will be people there to meet that you don't already know, and other places where you are just going about your normal workday, or a day of running errands, or taking care or personal matters, when you will see people you can interact with and meet.

New/Occasional Places You Shop

If you are looking for a place to get started encountering and meeting people that you don't already know, start by going to new stores or visiting ones that you go to on an infrequent basis.

Do this for a repair, to locate new sources of supply for yourself when the stores you regularly use don't have what you need, because you happen to be near a new store and it is convenient to stop in, or for items that you don't require except once or twice a year.

Also, make sure that you are familiar with the stores in your general market area and vicinity that you might mention to your customers when they have a need.

This type of contact is different from having a relationship with a clerk, manager, shopkeeper, or owner of an establishment because you stop in there regularly and you know each other by first name. We covered these types of contacts in the last chapter.

Here, we are looking for engaging and talking with people that you are seeing for the first time.

Remember it's just about the introduction. Your primary reason for visiting that store is to acquire a product or solution for a real need that you have. Your secondary objective is to meet someone new.

While you have regular places that you visit for your morning routine, lunch, and other services you require, make it a point once or twice a week — especially if you are driving in that area or going to be nearby — to visit a new establishment.

Depending on the number of other people in the store at the time and how occupied the clerk is handling other business, you may not have a chance to actually introduce yourself without it seeming forced or awkward. That's OK — save it for the next time, and plan a return visit to that store. Then you can reference the previous visit.

Depending on the type of store or business you visit, you may encounter a **clerk** working behind the counter or in the aisles. You might meet the **owner**, **proprietor**, **shopkeeper**, or **manager** (store manager, assistant manager, customer service manager, shift manager, crew chief, department head, or assistant department head). Occasionally, a district manager, someone from the home office, or a manager from another store will be visiting that store or helping out for the day. If it's a repair or technology business, you might meet a **technician or mechanic**.

You also might see **vendors** in the store — stocking shelves, replenishing merchandise, creating a display, or staffing a kiosk.

Then, there may be **other shoppers** in the store, just like you, that you can engage as you be look at the same product or type of product and ask each other's opinion or experience with that particular item.

These are places you might go once, twice, a few times a year where you are going to see all or some new faces each visit — unlike places you shop occasionally where there is not a lot of turnover by the staff and you see and speak with the same people from visit-to-visit.

When you consider that you could visit a store or business several times — particularly one with a lot of foot traffic — and see at least one new person each time, you can see the tremendous potential this holds for generating new sales leads.

Without enumerating every single type or variety of store that you might visit to locate employees different from the places you regularly visit — or the people who shop there — here are some general categories to get you started.

Think of **repair/mending** services (appliances, toys, clothing, sporting goods, automotive, and technology), parts stores (small and large appliances, vehicles, machinery, and tools) **hardware/home improvement** stores, **paint/wallpaper and flooring** stores, **grooming** (barber, shoe shine, and nails) **dry cleaners, tailors/ alterations, sporting goods, apparel** stores (clothing, shoes, jewelry, accessories, seasonal, hobbies, and outerwear), **card/gift** shops, **bookstores/newsstands, office supplies, cell phones, printing, furniture/home décor, appliances** (small handheld to major home appliances), **vehicles** (cars, trucks, boats, motorcycles, and watercraft), and **postal/shipping** centers.

There's **food and beverage** in its many forms (coffee, donuts, fast food, bagel shop, convenience store/gas station, food trucks, kiosks, ice cream, restaurants, roadside stands, package stores, and bars) that you can visit where you usually don't go and where people don't know you.

There are so many gas stations that you can easily vary the ones you visit. postal and parcel delivery stores,

Governmental Activities

In the municipality or area (township or unincorporated area) where you live, there is some type of governmental structure that has **regular meetings** open to the public, **public hearings** on zoning and budget matters, **jury duty** that you may be summoned to do with total strangers, and various **elected and** appointed officials and staff positions (some of these people you may know, but others you won't) that you might interact with, such as purchasing licenses or permits, ordering inspections, or paying parking fines.

You might also get involved in serving on or working in a **political campaign** or **referendum issue** that will benefit your builder and new home community. There are many people you can meet this way who are outside your normal circle of interaction.

Organizations & Groups

You may belong to one or more business, professional, sales, marketing, mastermind, or civic **groups** where there are new people joining as **members,** people visiting as **guests** or **prospective members,** or where you don't know all of the existing members yet. You might even join a new group where everyone essentially is a stranger to you.

There are going to be elected and appointed **officers** in your group or **organization**, and likely there is a **staff** or **administration** of some type (depending on its size, reach, and structure).

You might even run for or hold an office yourself or serve on or head a **committee** or subcommittee.

Your group may have **community activities** that it

organizes and conducts, **recruiting drives**, **youth programs**, or other ways for you to meet people outside of the organization but connected to it through those outreach activities.

Schools & Education

Of course there are many people you remember from your own days of going to college, real estate school, and other coursework you have completed — as well as teachers, administrators, and parents at your children's school or schools. We addressed that in the last chapter.

However, begin thinking also of the many people that you don't already know (**instructors**, **administrators**, **staff**, **other professionals**), that you may have an opportunity to meet at business, sales training, or continuing education or professional development **classes, workshops, or seminars** you attend that are held outside your company.

In terms of your children's schools, there are so many **activities** and **events** throughout the school year where you can meet people you don't already know (**instructors, administrators, staff, other parents**), such as open houses, PTA (or similar) meetings, fund raisers, sporting events, plays, concerts, science fairs, and festivals (or practices, rehearsals, and planning sessions for them). You might even do **volunteer work** or serve on a **committee**.

From your college days, in addition to the people you know from your time in attendance there, there are many opportunities to meet new people (including **staff and teachers** who have started since your last visit) at **class reunions, homecoming activities, sporting events, volunteer work**, and other contact you have with your school. Much of this, plus **parent weekends**, applies to the schools where your children attend.

Chance Encounters In Public

This is where many of your opportunities will come from as you are just out in the world. This is the opposite of contacting your circle of contacts because here you won't know who you might be meeting an engaging until it happens.

For instance, you may have **parking lot encounters** as you walk toward a store you from where you parked your car and you spot someone parked close to you with a decal or license plate on their car — or wearing a tee shirt or hat of your favorite **sports team, hobby,** or **cause** — even if it a team or organization from outside your immediate area. If it's from a rival team, that's a conversation starter also.

As you are **walking** inside the mall going from store-to-store or going along the sidewalk downtown, you may encounter people similarly dressed in team apparel — or comment on something else that catches your attention, such as their dog, their children, or their non-sports related outfit. Maybe they drop something or otherwise need help that you can provide.

Maybe your chance encounter is a little more direct where the two of you have **accidental or incidental contact** — touching, bumping, or running into each other on foot or in your car (with no damage being done).

Public transportation (commuter train, plane, bus, taxi, tram, shuttle, or subway) is a place to see and meet people, as is **standing in line** at restaurants, for a concert, to purchase something, or even the checkout line at the store.

People looking for **directions** or trying to find a **lost pet** or something of value they misplaced may approach and stop you in traffic, at the gas station, on the street or sidewalk, or even while you're in your front yard or driveway.

Events such as **block parties** where you likely will know many of the people attending can still have guests and people **new to the neighborhood**.

Even at your home or sales center, you will occasionally meet a **substitute mail or parcel delivery driver** or have someone arrive to **install or repair** an appliance or device you ordered or already have.

Medical Services

As you make medical appointments and keep them, you will interact with **doctors and nurses** (when you don't use that office very often or are seeing them for the first time), office, clinic, laboratory, or hospital **staff and administration** (including technicians and assistants), and people that you encounter in the **waiting room** (provided they are well enough to carry on a conversation with you.

Along with these professionals and others you will meet, you likely will see people as you shop for or engage **medical/wellness supplies** (including vitamins and supplements as well as medical equipment), **pharmacists**, and **health insurance agents**.

You might **visit the hospital** to check on friends or family and meet staff that you see or people who also are visiting friends or family.

Real Estate & Related Services

You will know many of the real estate agents and other professionals who work in your neighborhood to close and process your sales and to help exiting residents market their properties. There may be some that you don't know, and when you venture beyond your community or neighborhood, there will be many more that you can meet.

Identify, seek out, intentionally visit **brokerage offices** in your local market to meet people you don't already y know (brokers, Realtors®, assistants, and office staff), **homes for sale** in your immediate area (those listed as well for sale by owner), **stagers** and others preparing homes to sell, **professionals** who work with homes in your area (appraisers, lenders, closing agents, home inspectors, and title companies), **moving companies** (both for people leaving and moving into your area), and **truck rentals** (for people who pack and move the personal property themselves).

Don't forget **commercial leasing offices** for nearby office space and stores (brokers, agents, and staffs) and **rental apartment complexes** (leasing office and maintenance personnel).

While not strictly a real estate function, get to know people at nearby **storage facilities** (boat and RV storage, marinas, warehouses, and mini-storage) that serve your area.

Miscellaneous Sales Activities

There are people and events that you will encounter outside of normal retail and service functions that you should meet and get to know. Usually it will be with a **salesperson** where you will have the interaction, but there is an opportunity to meet other **consumers** who are also present.

There are a variety of activities where you might meet people and develop a relationship over time. These include **personal property auctions** (auctioneer, seller, staff, and other attendees), **private property sales** (estate sales, garage sales, yard sales, items listed on Craigslist or similar forum), **group sales** (flea markets and bazaars), **fund-raisers** (car washes and bake sales), **private vehicle sales** (you or someone else selling or buying a car, boat, or other vehicle), and **solicitations** (telephone calls, emails, texts, mail, or door-to-door canvassing).

Contractors

Of course there are many contractors that your company uses to build and deliver a new home, and I expect that you will reach out to the ones you already know. New people can show up to the jobsite at any time, so you need to be prepared to meet and engage them also.

In addition to the **skilled tradespeople** (from many different trades and services), learn who you can contact in the **main office** (managers, business owners, office staff, and administrators).

Look at your **existing homeowners** as well who may be having work done, such as putting in a pool or fence (where it is allowed), renovations and repairs (including kitchen and bath makeovers), general remodeling and room additions, or landscaping and other exterior features.

There are many opportunities for you to engage people who actually have some type of hands-on experience in the homes that you build so that they are in a great position to refer people to you.

Recreational & Social Activities

If you are a regular participant in any type of sport, hobby, or exercise, you likely will know people that participate with you. We have already discussed this.

Still, there are going to be **new faces** that you see at the gym, on the trail, and other places you go for activity.

It doesn't all need to be physical activity. Many social events and group activities are a good opportunity to see people that you don't know. Consider such things as **entertainment venues** (amusement parks, theme parks, miniature golf, arcades, shooting ranges, movie theatres, festivals, fairs, and carnivals), **sporting events**, **performances** (plays, recitals, lectures, and concerts), **pets** (dog parks, dog shows, dog training, and pet shops), **guided tours** (boat, bus, walking tours of museums and attractions), **shows** (home, garden, plant, craft, trade, expos, exhibits, and product demonstrations), **parks** (boardwalks, campgrounds, public parks, and playgrounds), **socials** (church, school, and club dinners and socials), and **get-togethers** (open houses, parties, receptions, mixers, picnics, weddings, and dances). Of course, there are other possibilities also.

Strategic Businesses & Professionals

Some of the people that you are going to want to meet will be just because of their occupation (attorney, stock broker, or insurance sales, for instance) or their physical office or business location in proximity to your new home community.

There might be one or more significant office buildings, shopping plazas, medical buildings, or other business centers near you that you will want to canvass to identify and meet as many (if not all) of the professional, business owners, managers, and key staff in those locations because their interactions with the public and their clientele could be quite beneficial to you.

This will take time and should be viewed as a long-term project, so don't rush it. Start with those who are available and easiest to contact first, and then go from there.

In making it a point to meet some of the people I have already identified in this chapter, you may have reached out to people in these major centers already. That's fine.

If not, here's another opportunity — based not on a common activity or business but on their location being close to your sales center.

Summary Of People You Can Meet

In the preceding pages, I have presented different types of individuals and situations where you can engage people, introduce yourself, and begin to develop those potential sales leads even though they were strangers to you up until you made that initial contact.

Some of the meetings and encounters you may plan for by specifically attending an event or going to someone's office. Others are just going to happen. The important thing is to be ready for them when they do happen and not shy away from them or try to make them more than they are. They are just the initial meeting and introduction — neither of you know this encounter was going to happen when and as it did.

Then, you can develop that contact and take it further after the initial meeting and conversation.

Here, in outline form are the many categories and types of individuals we just looked at in this chapter — people that you can engage by being open to the possibilities around you and intentionally being in places where people that you can meet are going to be.

This is not meant to be an exhaustive list, but it is extensive.

Next to each line item, you might mark whether this is someone that you intend to engage, or it's not high on your list right now. Nevertheless, this is your list, and this represents people that you can meet.

- **New/occasional places you shop**
  - **Clerks**
  - **Technicians/mechanics**
  - **Managers**
  - **Vendors**
  - **Other customers like you**
    - Florist and gift shops
    - Home improvement
    - Paint, wallpaper, and flooring stores
    - Home décor and design stores
    - Shipping or postage stores
    - Dry cleaning
    - Shoe repair
    - Appliance service or parts
    - Auto service (oil change, tire repair)
    - Emergency auto repair or towing service
    - Clothing (casual, play, dress, formal, seasonal, hobbies, sports, and outerwear)
    - Shoes and boots

- Jewelry and accessories
- Office supplies
- Automobile, RV, motorcycle, off-road vehicle dealer
- Automotive accessories
- Auto repair
- Boat and water craft dealer
- Sporting goods
- Warehouse clubs
- Printers, business cards, signs
- Bookstores and newsstands
- Technology, computer, and camera stores
- Furniture/home furnishings
- Grocery stores
- Convenience stores
- Liquor stores/wine shops
- Pharmacies
- "Back-to-School" or holiday shopping (Easter, Halloween, Christmas)
- Computer/camera/office equipment repair
- Gas station

- **Governmental activities**
  - **Regular members, officials, or attendees**
  - **Staff**
  - **Presenters**
  - **Visitors like you**

- Public hearings
- Regular meetings, such as City Council, School Board, and Zoning Board
- Building department, such as permitting and inspections
- Staff interaction
- Jury duty
- Purchasing licenses, paying parking fines
- Public open house
- Political campaigns for elected office or causes
- Political action/cause group

- **Organizations & groups**
  - **Officers**
  - **Staff and administration**
  - **Members**
  - **Volunteers**
  - **Other guests, prospective members, and visitors like you**
    - Mastermind or networking groups
    - Sales or marketing organization
    - Chamber of commerce, civic groups, charities/non-profits
    - Volunteer work sessions
    - Committee meetings
    - Recruiting drives

- Youth activities
- Hotels, conference centers, restaurants, clubs, and other venues

- **Schools & education**
  - **Teachers, coaches, and instructors**
  - **Staff and administration**
  - **Special events**
  - **Vendors**
  - **Volunteers**
  - **Other parents like you**
  - **Visitors and members of the public**
    - Open houses
    - Fund raisers and festivals
    - Sporting events
    - Plays and concerts
    - Science fairs and other exhibitions
    - Reunions, homecoming, parent weekends
    - Volunteers or committee service
    - Classes, lectures, and seminars
    - Continuing education/professional development classes

- **Public & chance encounters**
  - **Employees and staff**
  - **Officials**

- **Other members of the public like you**
    - Standing in line
    - Parking near or next to someone
    - Entering or leaving a store
    - Someone asking for information or directions
    - When you need assistance with your car, phone, or location
    - Riding on public transit (the commuter train, plane, bus, tram, shuttle, or subway
    - Accidental or incidental physical contact
    - New neighbors
    - Block party
    - Lost pet or personal property retrieval
    - Substitute parcel delivery or mail carrier
    - Merchandise/technology delivery, installation, service call, in-home set-up
- <u>Medical services</u>
    - **Doctors and other medical professionals**
    - **Staff and administration**
    - **Hospitals**
    - **Waiting room patrons**
    - **Medical supplies**
    - **Pharmacies**
    - **Health insurance**

- **Other members of the public**
    - Visits to medical facilities
    - Lab tests (such as blood tests, X-rays, and drug screening)
    - Offsite vaccines (flu shots, for instance)
    - Pharmacies (over-the counter, prescription medications, and first-aid supplies)
    - Vitamins and wellness products (grocery, pharmacy, or specialty store)
    - Visits to family or friends in the hospital
    - Durable medical equipment supplies
- **Real estate & related services**
    - **Brokers and Realtors®**
    - **Broker staff and administration**
    - **Appraisers**
    - **Lenders, loan processors**
    - **Inspectors, surveyors**
    - **FSBOs**
    - **Title companies, attorneys**
        - Brokerage offices in your local market
        - Homes for sale in your immediate area
        - Stagers and others preparing home to sell
        - Professionals who work with homes in your area
        - Moving companies (both people leaving and moving into your area)

- Mini-warehouse and storage facilities
- Moving companies
- Rental moving trucks and packing materials
- Commercial leasing agents
- Apartment complexes and leasing office

- **Miscellaneous sales activities**
  - **Private sellers**
  - **Salespeople**
  - **Managers or business owners**
  - **Staff and administration**
  - **Other customers or interested parties**
    - Personal property auctions
    - Estate sales, garage sales, yard sales
    - Flea markets, bazaars, car washes, bake sales
    - Selling or buying a car, boat, or any type of personal property (such as found in a Craigslist or newspaper ad)
    - Telephone, door-to-door solicitors

- **Contractors**
  - **Skilled tradespeople**
  - **Managers and business owners**
  - **Office staff and administrators**
  - **Laborers**

- Renovations and repairs
- General remodeling and room additions
- Kitchen and bath redesigns
- Landscaping, driveways, firepits, walkways, arbors, other exterior features
- Cabinetry, painting, and aesthetic improvements
- Heating, air conditioning, plumbing, electrical services
- Patios, pools, spas, water features

- **Recreational & social activities**
  - **Staff and employees**
  - **Managers**
  - **Exhibitors**
  - **Vendors**
  - **Volunteers**
  - **Visitors like you**
    - Amusement parks, theme parks, miniature golf, arcades, shooting ranges
    - Movie theatres
    - Ball games and sporting events
    - Plays, recitals, lectures, and concerts
    - Dog parks, dog shows, dog training, and pet shops
    - Walking, jogging, skating, bike riding

- Guided tours (boat, bus, walking), museums, and attractions
- Home, garden, plant, craft, and trade shows
- Festivals, fairs, expos, exhibits, product demonstrations, carnivals
- Campgrounds and marinas
- Public parks, playgrounds, ball fields, tennis courts, and boardwalks
- Golf courses, driving ranges, miniature golf
- Church, school, and club dinners and socials
- Open houses (of any type)
- Parties, receptions, mixers, picnics, weddings, dances
- Gyms, fitness centers, spas

- **Transportation services/facilities**
  - **Staff and employees**
  - **Managers**
  - **Vendors and suppliers**
  - **Patrons like you**
    - Rental cars
    - Limos
    - Tram/shuttles
    - Airports, train or bus stations, rental car counters
    - Waiting rooms at automotive service/oil change centers

- **Food & dining**
  - **Staff and employees (including wait staff and delivery drivers)**
  - **Managers/owners**
  - **Patrons like you**
    - Restaurants and fast food
    - Coffee shops
    - Food trucks
    - Street vendors/kiosks and roadside stands
    - Takeout/delivery
    - Banquets
    - Caterers
    - Food/wine tastings
- **Professionals to meet**
  - **Licensed professionals**
  - **Office staff and administration**
  - **Assistants and technicians**
  - **Waiting room patrons (like you)**
    - Doctors' offices, clinics, urgent care walk-in facilities
    - Optometrists and vision care
    - Dentists and dental care
    - Physical and emotional therapists
    - Pharmacists
    - Veterinarians.

- Accountants and bookkeeping services
- Attorneys and paralegals
- Notaries
- Insurance agents
- Financial planner
- People who do work in your home (pest control, pool service, cleaning)

6

Now What?

Having A Plan

As I have shown in the last two chapters, there are literally hundreds of people that you can reach out to as potential new home customers.

First you have to meet them (in the case of strangers) or let them know what you are doing and that at some point you'd like their help.

Then, regardless of whether they are people you already know or ones you will be meeting, you also want them to tell their friends and other contacts about your opportunity and refer them to you (indirectly by telling them about you or directly by telling you who they are and how to contact them).

It doesn't matter whether the people you are connecting with are initially known to you or not. You have two very large pools of potential customers from which to draw — those you already know and those you don't. Both groups could be quite large in size.

As I've mentioned, the number of people that you know in some way is fairly limited. At some point, you will have identified nearly all of the people you know (until you meet others), and then you will be depending on them introducing you to the people they know.

This is fine.

On the other hand, the number of people you haven't met yet that may have some interest in what you are offering (or may know other people who do) is a very large group of people — virtually limitless. You can always meet new people, and they will know other people that they can refer to you.

As you met new people and begin to develop a little bit of a relationship with them, they will transition into the "people you already know" category so that group of people will increase over time in this way.

Therefore, while your circle of people you know is rather finite, it continues to grow as you meet more people.

Nevertheless, you can't just go out into your marketplace in a few days and start talking to everyone you see or doing an email blast to everyone in your database. You must be strategic for your contact plan to work.

Putting Together A Plan

So you're going to need a plan.

This does not need to be an extremely detailed plan where you identify how many people you are going to contact each day and in what manner. It wouldn't work well that way even if it were your plan. You just can't count on or force opportunities to engage people.

However, you need to make a key decision to get started — also how you are going to approach your lead generation program.

Do you want to involve the people closest to you first by letting them know (the ones that don't already know) what you are doing and how you can use their help? Or, do you want to focus primarily on meeting new people and then let your friends and relatives know what you are doing as you see them?

Regardless of which method you select as your primary emphasis, it's not going to be a mutually exclusive one — just a way to get started. For instance, if you begin with family, close friends, and those you see on a regular basis, you likely will meet people as you are out and about in public.

You won't ignore those people or just go for a cursory introduction because they are not your main focus. Instead, you will welcome the opportunity to meet them as well, make the introduction, and set up a way to contact them again.

Likewise, if you are going to be building your database by reaching out to new contacts you will be making with strangers (rather than connecting with people you already know), you won't ignore the opportunity to mention what you are doing during a conversation with a friend or relative — even though you didn't plan on seeing or talking with them about your business until later.

It takes a unified, coordinated approach to add people to your database and get people interested in helping you. Just be open to all of the possibilities to meet and engage people — from close friends and relatives to total strangers that you will meet as you go through life.

Keeping Your Priorities Straight

As excited as you might be about generating new people to visit your sales center and allow you to talk with them about your new homes, you have to be a little patient. You have to lay the foundation first.

For the people you already know, they need to be aware of the fact that you are selling new homes, the types of homes you have, the general features you offer, the price point, and the location. You can't just expect that they will show up at your sales center — especially if they don't know where it is.

After you let your family. close friends, regular contacts, and casual acquaintances know what you're doing and how to contact you, you can begin to work on getting appointments and referrals. First, you need to make everyone aware of what you're doing and that you can use their help in some form.

Then, you can work on determining the type of help they can give you — from needing a new home themselves, telling you about a mutual acquaintance that is looking for a new home, mentioning a friend or contact of theirs that you don't know (and offering to tell them about you or giving you their contact information), or filing it away for future reference with no immediate plans to help you.

For the people you don't know that you are just meeting, the introduction is key. Sometimes that's all you'll be able to do on a quick, chance encounter. By getting at least a phone number from people you meet this way, you'll be able to contact them again and determine if developing a relationship is feasible.

Even when you are meeting people at their office or in a public place where longer conversations are possible, the introduction is still the way to begin. Then you can go for learning more about them and telling them more about you and your opportunity — depending on their interest level and willingness to help you.

Now It's Up To You

You have the opportunity to be a major source of new home sales center traffic you will receive in the future. Sure, passively generated traffic from a variety of print, online, broker, and signage sources will produce people for you to talk with, but you don't need to depend on this.

You have the ability to produce so much more — from people you already know as well as those you'll meet along the way. Make this an intentional lead generation program and not just something casual that you'll think of doing now and then.

You really have the power — and the strategies — for tapping into a very large potential of interested new home buyers.

Now, it's up to you to get started talking with the people you already know and meeting new people as you encounter them.

Steve Hoffacker

Steve Hoffacker, CAPS, MCSP, MIRM, is principal of Hoffacker Associates LLC, a sales training (new home sales, universal design, and aging-in-place) and coaching company based in West Palm Beach, Florida.

Steve is an award-winning, internationally-recognized and experienced new home salesperson and sales trainer, as well as a universal design/aging-in-place safety and accessibility sales trainer and instructor.

For more than 30 years, he has helped homebuilders, new home salespeople, contractors and remodelers, new home marketers, designers, architects, occupational therapists, and other professionals to be more visible, competitive, profitable, and effective — and to really enjoy themselves as they pursue their business and create wonderful customer experiences.

Steve wants you and your company to be successful and has created this guide (and many others) to help make that happen.

This book will be a great resource to help you take your business to another level and outpace the competition.

Use these strategies and concepts for your professional success.

www.ingramcontent.com/pod-product-compliance
Lightning Source LLC
Chambersburg PA
CBHW070920180426
43192CB00038B/2094